# The Journey In
# A Walk With Christ

## For New Believers

Trecia Lyn Davis

# Bible Quotes
All Scriptures mentioned are taken from the original King James Version (KJV) of the Holy Bible.

Copyright © 2025 by Trecia L Davis. All rights reserved.

The contents contained in this book may not be reproduced or distributed without prior written permission from author.

Independently published

**ISBN:** 979-8-218-71343-0

# Contents

Foreword

Acknowledgments

Dedications

Introduction

Chapter 1 - Beginners Guide

Chapter 2 - Desire For God

Chapter 3 - In The Beginning

Chapter 4 - If My People

Chapter 5 - Reverence

Chapter 6 - A Mustard Seed

Chapter 7 - The Holy Spirit

Chapter 8 - Finally Brethren

About The Author

# FOREWORD

Missionary Trecia Davis is a wonderful woman of God. Over the last several years, I've seen her grow up to be a mature woman of God. She loves the Lord, and this is evident in the life she lives.

This is a powerful piece for anyone who is seeking God. This book guides you from a baby in Christ to a believer who is now ready to go into spiritual maturity under the mighty hand of God, whereby you are taught to grow throughout the spiritual stages to become the Sons of God.

A must read!

**Prophet Sonia McKenzie**
Pastor, Open The Windows Of Heaven Ministry
Kendall, New York

# Acknowledgments

First, I must give honor and thanks to God, who is the head of my life, my guide and my source of inspiration. All glory to God! Truly grateful that He would work on the good desires of my heart, gracing me with the ability to write these few words. Thank you, Jesus. You've brought to fruition yet another dream of mine, and for that, I'm eternally grateful.

To my mother, Veta Davis, I hope you know your love for God, your strength, hard work, and dedication to family does not go unnoticed. Your support, love, and encouragement are treasured jewels forever etched in my heart.

To my pastors Albert and Marie Thompson, this book simply wouldn't be possible without you, your dedication to the things of God and those He placed in your care. After over 500 classes of Bible study that you rushed in from work to teach, know that you are appreciated and your labor is not in vain.

For all of my loved ones, my siblings, my two sons, my friends, and all the beautiful people God has sent in my life who encouraged me along the way, I thank God for you.

# Dedication

## In loving memory of Edward A. Davis, Sr

*To my earthly father, my daddy, known to many as Sonny, aka Barber, you are forever loved. You are greatly missed not only by me but also by our entire family.*

*With heartfelt gratitude, I thank you for the in-erasable impression and impact you had on my life. Your love for me always allowed and encouraged me to dream. Thank you for loving God enough and permitting me to go to church many a night a week as a young girl growing up. While out in the world, that foundation from childhood has been a guideline that kept me believing in God no matter what.*

*You were the first one in our family to go back to church and always led as the high priest in our home. You were the glue that kept us all together as one big happy family. Your love for Mommy will not allow me to settle. I see so much of you in me. I know if you were here, you would be my cheerleader and my biggest supporter, and you would be so proud to see me serving God. You always told me how special I am, and I trust you are smiling down on me, seeing it all come together.*

# Introduction

As I tarried at the altar at church to receive the infilling of the Holy Spirit, I had to get desperate enough to cry out for it.

I recall in that moment how determined I had to be in telling myself I had to have it. Nothing else in life seems to hold any level of importance in comparison to the Holy Spirit. Food at the time lost its flavor as I had a different type of appetite and hunger for more of God.

As I tarried at the altar, it was as if all my past mistakes and sins lined up on both sides of the longest road I've ever seen, as obstacles and people hindering my breakthrough. Way up ahead on that road, God was waiting for me, and I saw this entire scene play out like a movie in my mind.

When I saw as if the Lord was starting to turn and walk away, I was in despair! I instantly got down on bended knees both physically at the altar and spiritually on that road to get to God by any means necessary and to get His attention.

I was desperate and humble enough to crawl through the crowd of sin, guilt, shame, doubt, fear, and every barrier to go after God in an effort to receive the gift of the Holy Spirit. I knew I came in contact that night with Jesus.

When I eventually got up from the altar, I acknowledged something had miraculously changed in my life as I knew I got up with more power within that was never humanly possible. Also, the spirit was evident in me to some as I moved about under the anointing, interacting with others at the altar. There, I prayed for my mother and one of my biological sisters, who was also at the altar, all to the glory of God.

I went home that night and stayed up dancing, crying, and singing before the Lord as the work wasn't finished. The next morning, I went to church to meet with my pastors, as I had been led to do so the night before.

I was the first one at church as it was only my pastor, along with a minister and the woman of God from out of town, who was the speaker throughout the weekend services that were meeting up that morning, but I knew I was supposed to be there. As we were in the sanctuary praying, this is when the manifestation of me speaking with tongues came.

God is intentional, as He knew my pastors needed to bear witness to me receiving the infilling of the Holy Spirit with the initial evidence of tongues.

Honestly speaking, I originally thought this book would be a small Christian tract as I had a desire to find a way to encourage others to come to Jesus and to stay put in God. There's a burden in my heart to tell someone about Jesus and to show the way. I can never repay God for what He's done for me; however, if I can get one person to give their life to Jesus, it'll be my greatest accomplishment.

For those who are starting out, I pray for a deep personal relationship with God for you. The Bible says in Romans 8:19, "For the earnest expectation of the creature waiteth for the manifestation of the sons of God." Amen. This simply means that there are people out in this world, possibly you, who is reading this, that's waiting for servants of God such as myself to rise up, take our position, reach out, and share what we know.

Others have poured into me, and now I pour into you. Therefore, I hope this book finds such a one, and if that's you, I want you to know Jesus loves you, and if you give Him your heart, your life will never be the same.

For all of us, I pray we continually seek the Lord for more, giving Him our all as I truly believe the Word of God that tells us greater works we will do, basically as we continue on our journey with Almighty God.

We know the effectual fervent prayer of a righteous man availeth much. The Bible also clearly states there is none righteous. God points out that our righteousness is of Him.

I pray that God clothes me in his righteousness as I stand in agreement with you that the Lord will work on the good desires of your heart, bringing to pass all your dreams in Jesus' name, amen.

The cover of this book was inspired by the experience I had within my mind the night I got filled and had to press my way on what seemed to be a never-ending road that ultimately led to God.

I pray this book given to me by divine inspiration will encourage everyone who takes the time to read it to go after God in a more intimate way. Share with Him your dreams and aspirations.

This book touches on several significant factors that will assist you with living a victorious life as a child of God on your journey with Christ. There's the Beginners Guide that'll walk you through getting baptized in Jesus' name and joining a Bible-believing church. The other chapters speak of having a Desire for God, The Word of God, Prayer and Fasting, Worship, Faith, and chapter seven, Holy Spirit. The last chapter introduces The Armor of God.

I hope these few words act as a tool to get you going on your journey with our Creator and Savior, Jesus Christ.

# Chapter 1

# Beginners Guide

Somewhere along the way, you started getting tired of the everyday things and began to grow weary of the status quo. Even if you've acquired all the things this life has to offer, it is time for something different.

That is how God starts to speak to our hearts. For some of us, we had to deal with the loss of a loved one, the pain of a breakup, an abusive relationship, the loss of employment or home, difficulties raising children, or simply feeling unfulfilled.

There are also the fears associated with loneliness, divorce, depression, cancer, or any other illnesses that can happen at times, challenging our beliefs or lack thereof. You may have all you think is necessary, such as riches and all the material items, but there is a void. Everything the world has to offer can never fully satisfy. Our Creator fashioned us with this void so we can one day seek Him. Once we come to the realization of the emptiness inside, a longing deep within and thirstiness that only God can satisfy, we start seeking for more.

If you're reading this guide and have not yet addressed the yearning within or responded to God's nudging, then pause, listen and follow my instructions carefully. Jesus loves you! The Bible says in John 3:16, "For God so loved the world, that he gave his only begotten Son, that whosoever believeth in him should not perish, but have everlasting life." Also take a look at Jeremiah 1:5.

Please know, it does not matter where you have been or what you did in the past.

Even if you have committed murder salvation is still available to you. To become a believer, you must profess it by saying so with a sincere heart:

Lord Jesus, I accept You as my personal Lord and Savior. Humbly, I pray You forgive me of my sins and come into my heart, in Jesus' name, amen.

Now, the next step is just as crucially important, which is to find a Bible-believing church and get baptized in Jesus' name, as taught in the book of Acts chapter 2 verse 38, "And Peter said unto them, 'Repent and be baptized every one of you in the name of Jesus Christ for the forgiveness of your sins, and you will receive the gift of the Holy Spirit." Read also St. John 3:2-5. If you've answered the call, welcome; you are now a part of God's body (His people).

Let me just elaborate here for further understanding. Basically, baptism is a washing away of self while making a conscious decision (choosing) to live for God. You must repent and accept Jesus as your personal Lord and Savior. Water baptism is a symbol of doing away with the old you, burying, and being born again. Baptism, in Jesus' name, cleanses you of all your sins. In essence, going down in full immersion in water baptism gives you a fresh start. Do not be deceived by the enemy that let some think a sprinkling of water for baptism will suffice, for it is a lie.

After getting baptized in Jesus' name, you will need a Bible-believing church that can guide you in becoming a part of the body of Christ and learning the Word of God. For those that are brand new to the Christian walk, whenever you hear one say "in" followed by a foreign or unfamiliar word, it's often times referring to a book in the Bible.

One of the main functions of a Bible-believing church is that you will have a pastor who is considered to be a watchman over your soul, as referenced in Hebrews 13:17. In your pursuit of a Bible- believing church, please ensure it's a church that believes in the "five fold ministries" mentioned in Ephesians 4:11-16.

I cannot imagine how lost I would have been if it weren't for my pastor's guidance and teaching, as well as those of the prophets of God who's been instrumental in my understanding of my own gifting. I know the importance of a true church with leaders (Pastors) that truly live for God.

I was living in Florida at the time when I first met my now pastor, which is an answered prayer. I encourage you to pray and ask God, as I did, to lead you to a true Bible-believing church and the pastor that is right for you. Jeremiah 3:15 states, "And I will give you pastors according to mine heart, which shall feed you with knowledge and understanding."

Do not want to jump ahead here, but when you begin to read the Bible, you will quickly realize you need assistance in understanding it. Of course, the Holy Spirit, another must-have, will guide you in understanding, but it's also a part of your pastor's function. My pastor's Wednesday night Bible study plays a pivotal role in my Christian walk as a new believer and even until this day.

The church is affectionately called the Bride of Christ, as Jesus is the bridegroom. In the church, you will find other believers referred to as your brothers and sisters. They are considered to be your church/kingdom family. Now, I must make mention of the fact that the church is made up of broken people, imperfect people, coming to a perfect God so that He can perfect us. Let no one deter you from going to church. With your church family, you can worship God together, pray, serve, and encourage each other. Scripture backs this up, thus making a great topic to research along the way!

The church is referred to as the Body of Christ to depict the unity needed for us to operate effectively.

No different than the human body, with many parts working together, keeping the body alive and functioning. Read Romans 12:4-5.

Notice earlier, after baptism, I welcome you as a part of God's body. You, your brothers, your sisters (other believers) in Christ, and your pastor make up the body. This is your church community.

The Bible in Matthew 18:19-20 says, "Again I say unto you, That if two of you shall agree on earth as touching any thing that they shall ask, it shall be done for them of my Father which is in heaven." This lets us know we need other believers, as verse 20 goes on to say that where two or three are gathered together in my name, there am I in the midst of them. We need community to help us grow and understand how to live a purposeful life that pleases God. The church will aid in your development and can help you discover your purpose in life.

The Bible says God knew us from before we were formed in our mother's womb. So even when we think we know what our purpose in this life is, we may be pleasantly surprised once we make our way back to our Creator that there's a deeper calling on our lives. There's something in the body of Christ for every one of us to do. This is another inquiry to make a note of, asking God what He will have for you to do.

The Bible tells us in Psalm 100:4, "Enter into his gates with thanksgiving, and into his courts with praise: be thankful unto him, and bless his name."

We can come into the church with our worship and praise, blessing the name of the Lord. In church, we have fellowship. I strongly suggest you join a Bible-believing church as your life will be better for it, and so will your walk with Christ.

# Chapter 2

# Desire for God

A needed essential to help you on your way begins with a desire in your heart to know our Lord and Savior. Stop and think, "Who is better to know but the one that created you?" God knows you better than you know yourself. This reminds me of the Scripture in Matthew 10:30 which states, "But the very hairs of your head are all numbered." This verse reveals no one else will ever know you any better than your Heavenly Father no matter how hard they try. The most important, dare I say, the best thing my pastor ever told me was to have a personal relationship with God. My personal relationship with God has been a game-changer in my life.

Our Creator has many names. Throughout Scripture God is referred to as the I Am, Yahweh, Adonai, Elohim, Jehovah, LORD, Abba Father, Immanuel, Alpha and Omega, El Roi, Holy Messiah, El-Shaddai, Jesus, El Elyon, and Jehovah Jireh to name a few. You can gain insights as to who God is by studying his names.

I encourage you to get to know the God of the Bible and to know Him intimately. God works on the good desires of our hearts, so let there be a desire to know Him more and more. Study Him, learn His ways and what He requires of us as His people, in essence, just draw close to Him. Find out what breaks God's heart and what brings Him joy.

The Bible says we can become a friend of God. He can be all we can ever ask or need. John 15:13 states, "Greater love hath no man than this, that a man lay down his life for his friends."

God is a friend, a companion, a guide, a father to the fatherless and mother to the motherless, a counselor, a burden bearer, a shelter in the time of storm, a provider, a protector, a healer, a deliverer, a comforter, master, redeemer, savior, defender, way maker, and so much more.

Fall in love with Jesus. He tells us in His Word if we love Him, we must obey His commandments so we can please Him. How can we be a friend to God? According to John 15:14, "Ye are my friends, if ye do whatsoever I command you." This means we must also find out His commandments!

Talk to God as if you are corresponding with a friend who is right there because He hears us as if He's sitting right next to us. Ask God to give you ears to hear Him when He speaks.

God is all-knowing and has all power. Scripture tells us Jesus went to the cross at Calvary, where He bled and died in our stead. He was innocent, and we were guilty, but He paid the price for us, letting them nail Him to the cross and crucify Him so He could redeem us of our sins. He was buried but rose triumphant on the third day with all power, conquering death, hell, and the grave.

There is no love greater than the love of God. Let me repeat: there is absolutely no love greater than the love of God. His talk is not cheap, as He suffered for us. The Bible says in Numbers 23:19, "God is not a man, that he should lie; neither the son of man, that he shall repent: hath he said, and shall he not do it? or hath he spoken, and shall he not make it good?" If He says it, you can bank on it. His promises are sure. The God we serve knows every hair on our heads. Don't you want a friend that truly cares for you? I've never met an individual who answered no.

Our father is a confidant that you can go to about any and everything. One you can truly be yourself with as He is our Creator.

Here's a little food for thought: What are you willing to sacrifice for a closer walk with God?

Seek an intimate relationship with Him; it's a closeness like nothing you've ever experienced before. It is possible with GOD and yours for the taking!

# Chapter 3

# In the Beginning

A Bible, preferably a hard copy of the King James Version known as KJV, is another necessity to teach you the Word of God. To note there are several versions of the Bible available today; however, I still recommend your first and main Bible to be the KJV. You can choose to have another version in addition to your KJV as a cross-reference or as a backup. There is also the Bible app to have on your phone to access the Word of God when you do not have your physical Bible with you.

John 1:1-3 states, "In the beginning was the Word, and the Word was with God, and the Word was God. The same was in the beginning with God. All things were made by him; and without him was not any thing made that was made." Amen. Right here, we see why we can throw the Big Bang theory and all the other unproven suggestions out the window as to who created what. Getting to know the written Word helps you to know God as the Word is God.

As you dive into the Bible, you will come across words perhaps you have never heard of before, and that's ok. Some of these words will be rather challenging to pronounce, but I say read it anyway.

As a new believer, my personal opinion is that you need to read the Bible whether you understand or not. To me, it is like eating vegetables, you do not necessarily see what it is doing for you right away, but you trust that it is making you better. So it is with the Word of God. Reading the Word of God is nourishment to your soul.

Previously, I mentioned you will need assistance in comprehending the Word of God. This is where my pastor and church comes in. I am blessed to be a part of a Bible-believing church where my pastor teaches and preaches the undiluted Word of God.

He not only preaches the Word in the sanctuary on Sundays, but we also have a prayer line that gives us additional avenues to fellowship, where my pastor and co-pastor, along with other leaders, get to bring forth the Word of the Lord. Then there is my beloved Wednesday night Bible study that has left an indelible impression on me, which I can see clearly as these words flow from my soul into this book. For that, I am grateful.

Absorb the Word of God as much as you take in the natural food, and watch your life be transformed. You can read the Holy Word to find strength and peace and to familiarize yourself with the gentle, loving, yet mighty God we serve. Studying the Bible teaches us what God requires of us. For example, Psalm 119:11 tells us to hide His Words in our hearts so that we do not sin against Him (paraphrased version).

Your church/kingdom family will contribute to your overall growth as you participate by attending different services and workshops throughout your community. Once you know God has connected you to the right leaders, you can follow them as they follow Christ. Your pastors will affiliate themselves with other houses of worship that they know are living for God.

I start every day with prayer first, then audibly read a few Scriptures from my Bible and read a daily devotional. A devotional is another item that will aid in your understanding of the Gospel and spiritual growth.

I will briefly touch on the whole armor of God, and hopefully, I will revisit this later in the book. The Lord has given us spiritual weapons as we are in a war, but it is a spiritual one.

Please rest assured that God fights all our battles, so know that the fight is fixed with whatever fighting we have to do.

Saying this to say our only offensive weapon is the sword of the Spirit, which is the Word of God. This can be found in Ephesians 6:17. I suggest when reading your Bible to read aloud. We can use the Word by knowing and believing while speaking the Word to disarm the devil and stop him in his tracks.

# Chapter 4

# If My People…

Prayer is required, and so it is imperative that you develop a prayer life. A prayer life is being in constant communication with God. Prayers grant us that access, enabling us to reach out to the Lord no matter the time of day or night.

Prayer changes things! 2 Chronicles 7:14 states, "If my people, which are called by my name, shall humble themselves, and pray, and seek my face, and turn from their wicked ways; then will I hear from heaven, and will forgive their sin, and will heal their land." Amen.

Praying serves as a way to build your connection or relationship with God, and like any other successful relationship, communication is key. Real intimacy with God requires consistency. You do not have to pray long prayers. I recommend daily prayers. It is said that it takes 21 days to form a habit, so if you pray daily for the next month or 30 days, you will have already developed a prayer life. You can start by simply closing your eyes and having a heart-to-heart with the Most High God.

The Bible states in 1 Thessalonians 5:17 to pray without ceasing. Amen. Constant prayer with the Lord is not limited to an outward cry or an audible speech but can also include sitting in silence before Him, listening, and allowing Him time to speak or praying within.

The Bible encourages us to pray for one another in James 5:16, and this Scripture also tells us that the effectual fervent prayer of a righteous man availeth much. My co-pastor always says, "If you want to see your kids blessed, pray for other people's children," and I have adapted and proven this principle along the way.

Quick testimony of the goodness of God and taking Him at His Word. Many years ago, the young people in my church were all going away to the annual youth camp for a couple of days like they normally do. I did not have the means at the time to send my son. Back then, I oversaw a midweek prayer in church on Wednesday mornings, where a handful of us would meet and pray. I was alone in the sanctuary on this particular day, or so I believed. As I usually do, I dropped the mothers back home and came back to clean the church. I had come to grips with the fact that I could not afford to send my son to camp. However, this did not deter me from praying for those who were getting ready to go. I prayed fervently on bended knees for them to get there safely, have a wonderful time, and for someone to be filled with the Holy Spirit.

Almost immediately after praying, while I was still kneeling at the altar, my co-pastor called and offered to pay for my son to attend camp.

Look at my Heavenly Father making a way when I did not even ask Him to help. I was blown away by what a mind-blowing, on-time, way-making God I serve. I could not help but give Him glory! My son went to camp and returned filled with the Holy Spirit; he has never been the same after the camp. All glory to God. Needless to say, prayer changes things, and our God is a prayer-answering God.

Reach out to your leaders if you are in a church that can connect you with trusted brethren who can come together in prayer. Suggest starting a prayer line if you end up in a church that does not have one. There is power in prayer and in praying with others. Praying for strength and forgiveness along the way is vital to your happiness, growth, and overall well-being as a new believer.

Side note: If you dream like I do, prayer is where you bring your dreams before the Lord so He can give you the revelation and interpretation of the dreams. This helps you to know how to pray as led regarding your dreams. Sometimes, your dream reveals an answer to your prayer.

Prayer is fundamental. You would not believe how many times prayer has saved me from making wrong decisions, stopped me from heading in the wrong direction, and prevented me from going places and doing things that would profit me nothing.

Also, keep a pen and paper handy wherever you pray, should you feel led to jot something down. There will be times when you will get divine inspiration and or revelation and need to write it down.

As a point of reference, I will leave you with the prayer that Jesus gave His disciples after they asked Him to teach them how to pray. Also known as the "Lord's Prayer."

Taken from Luke 11:2-4, "And he said unto them, When ye pray, say, Our Father which art in Heaven, Hallowed be thy name. Thy kingdom come. Thy will be done, as in Heaven, so in earth. Give us day by day our daily bread. And forgive us our sins; for we also forgive every one that is indebted to us. And lead us not into temptation; but deliver us from evil." Amen.

It is necessary to point out that prayer should sometimes be paired with fasting. This is where we must also crucify our flesh. Not to jump ahead, but bear in mind that within us, there is a war between our flesh and our spirit. Now, what is fasting?

From a Christian perspective, fasting is refraining from food and drink for a specific amount of time in an effort to draw closer to God. Personally, I have included abstaining from TV and all social media platforms at times and even trying to lessen my interaction with others as best I can while fasting.

A Scripture verse that immediately comes to my mind is Joel 1:14, "Sanctify ye a fast, call a solemn assembly, gather the elders and all the inhabitants of the land into the house of the Lord your God, and cry unto the Lord."

Then there is Joel 2:12, "Therefore also now, saith the Lord, turn ye even to me with all your heart, and with fasting, and with weeping, and with mourning."

The book of Ezra 8:23 states, "So we fasted and besought our God for this: and he was entreated of us."

If you are married, I will leave this passage of Scripture with you so you know how to conduct yourself as it relates to prayer and fasting. 1 Corinthians 7:5 reads, "Defraud ye not one the other, except it be with consent for a time, that ye may give yourselves to fasting and prayer; and come together again, that satan tempt you not for your incontinency."

We see that fasting is mentioned throughout Scripture. Fasting is established in the Word of God as an essential tool to ask of God, get His attention, and allow us to hear Him clearer, especially since we always need His guidance.

Fasting goes hand in hand with prayer. Get in the habit of inquiring of the Lord with prayer and fasting before making any major decisions, as not doing so can be detrimental to your journey with Christ.

You should have a personal day where you fast. Corporate fasting is a time of coming together with your church or other believers to seek the Lord, and you should have a day for this as well, as there is strength in numbers.

Prayer and fasting will help you to know God's voice so you know who is speaking, as we aim to be obedient to the voice of the Lord.

God's guidance is paramount as we journey with Him, so I will close with a Scripture I often think of daily, taken from Proverbs 3:5-6 that says, "Trust in the Lord with all thine heart; and lean not unto thine own understanding. In all thy ways acknowledge him, and he shall direct thy paths."

# Chapter 5

# Reverence

A greatly needed essential is worship, which is defined as the feeling or expression of reverence and adoration for a deity. Biblically, worship means grateful submission to God.

To me, worshipping God starts with a heart of gratitude. Start with a simple opening of the mouth professing one's love for the Lord, considering who He is, for the joy and peace He gives when needed. John 4:24 states, "God is a spirit, and they that worship him must worship him in spirit and in truth."

1 John 4:19 says, "We love him because he first loved us." Us, who can make mistakes and fall short and need His help and forgiveness, yet He loves us even though we are not deserving. Our Creator loved us long before we even acknowledged Him, making God worthy of all our worship.

Just like prayer, worship comes in many forms. We can worship God by living a life pleasing unto Him so He can be like a proud parent.

Revelations 19:1 says, "And after these things I heard a great voice of much people in heaven, saying, Alleluia; Salvation, and glory, and honor, and power, unto the Lord our God:"

Worshipping God in the here and now prepares us as there will be great worship in Heaven throughout all eternity.

We can worship the Lord in various ways, including kneeling, bowing in reverence to His holy name, or blowing Him a kiss as adoration unto Him. Additionally, we can worship God by praising, dancing, singing, crying out with a heart of gratitude, and raising our hands to give Him glory and honor. Read Psalm 150 in its entirety.

One of my favorite little chapters in the Bible is Psalm 100 and its 5 verses, which is known as a psalm of praise. This is a great starting point to learn Scripture and what God requires of us, whether we are coming before Him at home, in church, or wherever. Whichever way you choose to worship the Almighty God, just remember who you are going before and honor Him from that place. When it comes to worshipping Him, make it personal and authentic.

Psalm 100:1-5, "Make a joyful noise unto the LORD, all ye lands. Serve the LORD with gladness: Come before his presence with singing.
Know ye that the LORD he is GOD: It is he that hath made us, and not we ourselves; We are his people, and the sheep of his pasture.
Enter into his gates with thanksgiving, And into his courts with praise: Be thankful unto him, and bless his name.
For the LORD is good; his mercy is everlasting; And his truth endureth to all generations." Amen.

This is all worship!!

# Chapter 6

# Mustard Seed

Faith is another vital foundational necessity. To have faith is to have a strong belief in God, trusting in Him completely. I am particularly passionate about faith as my journey has been one that has required great faith and, in return, has given me many testimonies.

There are a few Scriptures regarding faith to know and apply on your journey with Christ as a new believer. The book of Hebrews 11:1 defines faith as, "Now faith is the substance of things hoped for, the evidence of things not seen." This is where a healthy imagination can come in handy. Having the ability to dream and visualize works wonders as it relates to faith. Faith, however, does require a lot of patience, as there's a lot of waiting at times while you're standing in faith.

Hebrews 11 lists several examples of faith throughout its 40 verses. In verse 6, it speaks of how impossible it is to please God without faith, thus reinforcing how crucial faith is in the life of a child of God.

The Bible says in Matthew 17:20, "If ye have faith as a grain of mustard seed, ye shall say unto this mountain, Remove hence to yonder place; and it shall remove; and nothing shall be impossible unto you."

Well, my sister, a chef at the time, bought some mustard seeds and showed me just how tiny they are. Another big sis in faith brought me my own mustard seed to have, and I cannot tell you how I studied that little seed. Made me recognize how small yet solid, whole, and complete it is.

Faith must be complete just like the little mustard seed, leaving no room for doubt.

Faith will be needed to walk with God, live for Him, serve Him, and be used by Him. Take, for example, when you pray and ask God for something, or He makes a promise to you, then you have to wait, believing that He will do what He says He will do. Sometimes, a prayer can be answered instantly, while other times, a promise may take several years to come to pass. These are moments where your faith will be tested, and if you are not careful, you will find yourself questioning and saying, "Did God really say that?" Faith demands confidence in God, and Scripture tells us that He is not like man that He should lie, so if God said it, you can take that to the bank as it is guaranteed.

Find ways to grow your faith. Take baby steps in putting God to the test. For example, the Bible says He works on the good desires of our hearts.

The Bible also states, "Ask, and it shall be given; knock and it shall be open unto thee." Try being strategic and specific, asking for a small favor like waking you up at a certain time or having someone specific reach out to you.

Make a note of it when it happens, and it will encourage you to trust God more and more. I recommend that you audibly read Psalm 23 daily, believing by faith, and watch your life be transformed. Faith is surely a needed essential that will help you foster an intimate relationship with God.

# Chapter 7

# The Holy Spirit

What I am about to say, I simply cannot say strongly enough. You will need the infilling of the Holy Spirit, and let no one tell you any different. God is a Spirit, as found in St John 4:24. It is declared throughout Scripture that the Holy Spirit is God. It is critical you ask God immediately to fill you with His Holy Spirit and with fire. To note: Holy Spirit and Holy Ghost mean exactly the same thing. Holy Ghost is also called "The Comforter."

In the beginning, after the fall of men, sin caused us to be separated from God, but once we turn and acknowledge Him then His desire will be to live in us. The infilling of the Holy Spirit is an act of surrender, allowing God to govern over your life, letting His presence take up residence within you.

As a believer, the Holy Spirit is promised to us. The infilling of God's Holy Spirit is a gift from Him that He freely gives. Romans 8:9 reads, "But ye are not in the flesh, but in the spirit, if so be that the spirit of God dwell in you. Now if any man have not the Spirit of Christ, he is none of his." Amen. Basically telling you it is vitally important that you get the infilling of God's Holy Spirit. You must be in a place, however, where you can receive it, and I'm not referring to a physical location. Your heart must be in a place where you can invite God in to come and take up residence.

Luke 11:13 states, "If ye then, being evil, know how to give good gifts unto your children: how much more shall your heavenly Father give the Holy Spirit to them that ask him?" Clearly, Scripture is telling us here that one of the ways in which you can aid in your receiving of the Holy Spirit is to ask God for it. Some other way is to pray earnestly to receive it.

Stay in a place of expectancy. Attend all the services your church has to offer, but also know you can get filled at home as well. Get to know God through reading His Word and worship Him along the way.

Get around like-minded believers who can intercede on your behalf and worship the Lord with you. This is also biblical according to Acts 2:1-4, which reads, "And when the day of Pentecost was fully come, they were all with one accord in one place. And suddenly there came a sound from Heaven as of a rushing mighty wind, and it filled all the house where they were sitting. And there appeared unto them cloven tongues like as of fire, and it sat upon each of them. And they were all filled with the Holy Ghost, and began to speak with other tongues, as the Spirit gave them utterance." Amen.

Acts 4:31 reads, "And when they had prayed, the place was shaken where they were assembled together; and they were all filled with the Holy Ghost, and they spake the word of God with boldness."

Ephesians 5:18 informs us to be filled with the Spirit. I make mention of all these Scriptures to ensure that you seek after it. The Bible says no good thing will He withhold from them that diligently seek Him. Also, it does not matter how long it takes you to get filled, whether a day, a week, a month, a year, or two; just know it's yours for the taking.

In case it takes you some time to receive the infilling of the Holy Spirit, let it not discourage you, as it also took me a very good while.

However long it takes you to receive the infilling of the Holy Spirit or anything that God has for you, exercise your faith believing, and know that it is worth the wait.

# Chapter 8

# Finally Brethren

Finally, my brethren, be strong in the Lord and in the power of His might.

Put on the whole armour of God, that ye may be able to stand against the wiles of the devil.

For we wrestle not against flesh and blood, but against principalities, against powers, against the rulers of the darkness of this world, against spiritual wickedness in high places.

Wherefore take unto you the whole armour of God, that ye may be able to withstand in the evil day, and having done all, to stand.

Stand therefore, having your loins girt about with truth, and having on the breastplate of righteousness;

And your feet shod with the preparation of the gospel of peace;

Above all, taking the shield of faith, wherewith ye shall be able to quench all the fiery darts of the wicked.

And take the helmet of salvation, and the sword of the Spirit, which is the word of God:

Praying always with all prayer and supplication in the Spirit,...

This entire page is taken from the Bible in Ephesians chapter 6, verses 10-18.

Ephesians 6 describes how to posture yourself as a believer, knowing you are in a fight for your very life but, more importantly, your soul.

The good news in this particular passage of Scripture is that you have a God given armour you can rely on. Teaching you, that it is not a physical fight against others, but rather a spiritual one against forces of darkness and that you have been given protective gear to stand and safeguard yourself, from the schemes of the enemy. This is spiritual warfare.

A well-known tactic of the enemy is to plant doubt and fear, which is why God's instructions are to be strong in Him and believe in His power.

Another strategy of the devil is to study your behavior, looking for fractures in your armour. Therefore, utilize the shield of faith, moving it around, extinguishing all the darts being sent your way. The enemy will attempt to attack your mind with lies, confusion and accusations. However, do not be discouraged. Be proactive in putting on the helmet of salvation. Always know who you are, remembering that you now belong to God.

It is important to take the sword of the spirit, which is the word of God and your only offensive weapon. Employ the Word letting the enemy know it is defeated in Jesus' name. Make use of Isaiah 54:17 declaring it daily, which states, "No weapon that is formed against thee shall prosper; and every tongue that shall rise against thee in judgment thou shalt condemn. ..." According to 1 Thessalonians 5:17, we are to "Pray without ceasing." Ask Him for protection, strength, healing, deliverance, victory and whatever is needed at any given moment. Bring all your requests before the Lord.

Once you have armed yourself with the necessary essentials mentioned in this book, you can confidently journey along in your walk with Christ.

As you follow Jesus you'll gain your own experiences, your own testimonies and hopefully your own divine encounters with Almighty God. All for His glory.

Let us, therefore, stand in faith, in victory, knowing in the end, we win. The celebration for enduring to the end will be in Heaven, and I hope to see you there!

Remember, as you learn, share. We are in this together. Stronger together. Each one should show another the way!

# Missionary Trecia Lyn Davis
## Author

Trecia L. Davis passionately loves the Lord. She is easily described as strong, loyal, and always willing to lend a helping hand. Since she was born in Kingston, Jamaica, she's often referred to as "Likkle but she talawah," a Jamaican term meaning small, strong, and not to be underestimated.

Trecia is an ordained missionary who serves in many ways in her local church. She is the Women's President. She also serves in hospitality and usher ministries. Her love for God and passion for helping others are the driving forces that afford her the time to serve the community at large via her church's food pantry.

Although she often doesn't say much, Trecia hopes the modesty, faith, and servitude she exemplifies will aid as a guide and blueprint for her peers, the ladies she serves as Women's President, as well as those coming up after her.

This chosen vessel of God takes great joy in being a mother to her two sons, Dymetre and Demaar. Being a single mother for twenty-plus years and seeing the blessings of the Lord unfold in her life in the various ways He's shown up and kept her is her overall testimony that nothing is impossible with God.

www.ingramcontent.com/pod-product-compliance
Lightning Source LLC
Chambersburg PA
CBHW070951180426
43194CB00041B/2044